THE CUBAN MISSILE CRISIS

PETER CHRISP

WORLD ALMANAC® LIBRARY

Please visit our web site at: www.worldalmanaclibrary.com
For a free color catalog describing World Almanac® Library's
list of high-quality books and multimedia programs,
call 1-800-848-2928 or fax your request to (414) 332-3567.

Library of Congress Cataloging-in-Publication Data

Chrisp, Peter.
    The Cuban Missile Crisis / by Peter Chrisp.
      p. cm. — (The Cold War)
    Includes bibliographical references and index.
    Contents: On the brink — Cold warriors — Revolutionary Cuba — Cold warfare — Khrushchev's missile gamble —
Reacting to the missiles — The blockade — A peaceful solution? — Lessons of the crisis.
    ISBN 0-8368-5273-7 (lib. bdg.)
    ISBN 0-8368-5278-8 (softcover)
    1. Cuban Missile Crisis, 1962—Juvenile literature. [1. Cuban Missile Crisis, 1962. 2. United States—Foreign relations—
Soviet Union. 3. Soviet Union—Foreign relations—United States. 4. World politics—1955-1965.] I. Title. II. Series.
E841.C49   2002
973.922—dc21   2001046605

This North American edition first published in 2002 by
World Almanac® Library
330 West Olive Street, Suite 100
Milwaukee, WI 53212 USA

This U.S. edition © 2002 by World Almanac® Library. Original edition published in Great Britain
in 2001 by Hodder Wayland, a division of Hodder Children's Books. Additional end matter
© 2002 by World Almanac® Library.

Series concept: Alex Woolf
Editor: Joanna Bentley
Designer: Derek Lee
Consultant: Scott Lucas, Head of American and Canadian Studies, University of Birmingham
Proofreader: Serena Penman
Map illustrator: Nick Hawken
World Almanac® Library designer: Scott M. Krall
World Almanac® Library editor: Jim Mezzanotte
World Almanac® Library production: Susan Ashley and Jessica L. Yanke

Picture credits: AKG: 24, 48, 53, 54; Camera Press: cover; Christian Science Monitor: 49; Consolidated News
Pictures: 9; Bettmann/Corbis: 16, 38, 51; James Davies, Eye Ubiquitous/Corbis: 58; Eye Ubiquitous: 56; Imperial
War Museum: 8; Peter Newark's American Pictures: 13, 14, 23, 31; Photri: 44; Popperfoto: cover, 7, 11, 19, 21, 22,
28, 30, 32, 34, 47, 59; Topham Picturepoint: 12, 25, 33, 35, 37, 40, 41, 46; United Nations: 50; Wayland Picture
Library: cover, 6, 20, 52

Quotation Sources: *Khrushchev Remembers* by Nikita Khrushchev (Sphere Books, 1971); *Kennedy v. Khrushchev, The Crisis
Years* by Michael R. Beschloss (Faber & Faber, 1991); *The Brink: Cuba, Castro and John F. Kennedy, 1964* by David Detzer
(J.M.Dent & Sons, 1970); *Fidel Castro Speaks* edited by Martin Kenner and James Petras (Penguin, 1969); *Robert Kennedy
and his Times* by Arthur M. Schlesinger Jr. (André Deutsch, 1978); *Eyeball to Eyeball*, BBC2 television series *Timewatch*,
1992; *Thirteen Days: A Memoir of the Cuban Missile Crisis* by Robert F. Kennedy (Macmillan, 1968); *The Kennedy Tapes:
Inside the White House during the Cuban Missile Crisis* edited by E.R. May and P.D. Zelikow (Harvard University Press,
1997); *On the Brink: Americans and Soviets Re-examine the Cuban Missile Crisis* by James G. Blight and David Welch (Hill
and Wang, 1989); *As I Saw It* by Dean Rusk (I.B. Tauris, 1991); *Back to the Brink: Proceedings of the Moscow Conference on
the Cuban Missile Crisis* edited by B.J. Allen, J.G. Blight, and D.A. Welch (University Press of America, 1992); *We Now
Know: Rethinking Cold War History* by John Lewis Gaddis (Oxford University Press, 1997); *The Cuban Missile Crisis Revisited*
edited by James Nathan (St. Martin's Press, 1992); *In Confidence* by Anatoly Dobrynin (Times Books, 1995); *Venceremos!
The Speeches and Writings of Che Guevara* edited by John Gerassi (Panther, 1972)

Printed in the United States of America

1 2 3 4 5 6 7 8 9 06 05 04 03 02

Contents

CHAPTER ONE

On the Brink

The month of October in the year 1962 was perhaps the most momentous period in all of human history. The world's two superpowers, the United States and the Soviet Union, stood on the brink of nuclear war. Each had the capacity to destroy not only each other but half the countries of the world.

Their quarrel was over the island of Cuba, a Soviet ally that lies just 90 miles (144 kilometers) from the coast of Florida. Photographs taken by U.S. spy planes showed that the Soviets were building nuclear missile sites in Cuba. Once installation was complete, the missiles would have the range and power to destroy every major U.S. city except Seattle, and there would be no defense against them.

U.S. president John F. Kennedy was determined to get the Soviet missiles out of Cuba, even if he had to risk a war between the United States and the Soviet Union to do so. He ordered a naval blockade to prevent Soviet ships from reaching Cuba. Eventually, over a hundred ships, nearly a thousand U.S. aircraft, and more than 100,000 U.S. troops were ready for conflict.

Waiting in Cuba was a Soviet army 42,000 strong, far larger than Kennedy had imagined. These Soviet troops were armed with tactical nuclear weapons, which they were prepared to use.

Range of Soviet Missiles from Cuba

Jet bombers - 700 miles (1,130 km)
(Atlanta, Miami, Central America)

Medium-range ballistic missiles - 1,000 miles (1,610 km)
(Washington D.C., Houston)

Intermediate-range ballistic missiles -
2,250 miles (3,620 km) (nearly all of United States)

◀ This map shows the range of attack that various Soviet weapons would have possessed if located in Cuba.

NUCLEAR ALERT

At the height of the Cuban missile crisis, U.S. forces were on alert at "defense condition two," the highest state of combat readiness short of actual war. All nuclear units were ordered to load their weapons and be ready for firing. Long-range B-52 bombers, loaded with nuclear bombs, took to the air and circled in readiness. The U.S. Navy sent Polaris submarines towards Soviet waters. Each submarine carried nuclear missiles with more destructive power than all the bombs dropped during World War II.

President Kennedy was always within a ninety-second reach of a black case, nicknamed the "football." This case held the codes that the president could use to unleash nuclear war. In underground bunkers, officers of the Strategic Air Command waited for his order.

"BY A THREAD"

Just as great as the chance that Kennedy or Soviet premier Nikita Khrushchev might intentionally start a war was the possibility that war would erupt through miscalculation or error. On October 27 a U.S. plane flew off course into Soviet airspace, giving the impression that an attack had begun. On the same day, in Cuba, a Soviet general decided on his own initiative to shoot down a U.S. plane.

"Nuclear catastrophe was hanging by a thread," Soviet general Anatoly Gribkov later recalled, "and we weren't counting days or hours, but minutes."

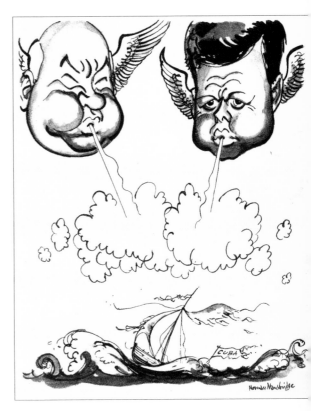

▲ In 1962, Cuba was a small country caught between two rival superpowers. This British cartoon shows the island as a little boat in a violent storm, blown in different directions by Khrushchev, on the left, and Kennedy on the right.

SLEEPING IN THE KREMLIN

In his memoirs, Soviet premier Nikita Khrushchev describes one night during the Cuban missile crisis:

"I spent one of the most dangerous nights at the Council of Ministers office in the Kremlin. I slept on a couch in my office — and I kept my clothes on ... I was ready for alarming news to come at any moment, and I wanted to be ready to react immediately."

KHRUSHCHEV REMEMBERS BY NIKITA KHRUSHCHEV

CHAPTER TWO

Cold Warriors

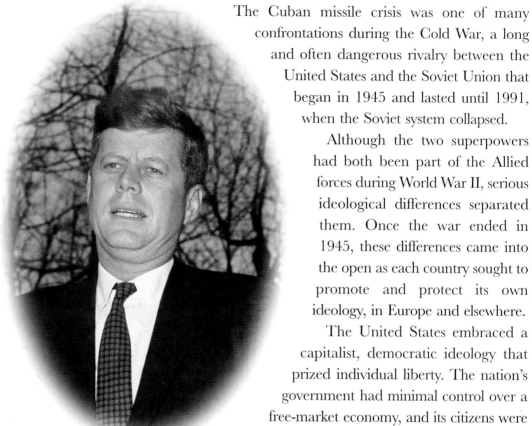

The Cuban missile crisis was one of many confrontations during the Cold War, a long and often dangerous rivalry between the United States and the Soviet Union that began in 1945 and lasted until 1991, when the Soviet system collapsed.

Although the two superpowers had both been part of the Allied forces during World War II, serious ideological differences separated them. Once the war ended in 1945, these differences came into the open as each country sought to promote and protect its own ideology, in Europe and elsewhere.

The United States embraced a capitalist, democratic ideology that prized individual liberty. The nation's government had minimal control over a free-market economy, and its citizens were free to own property, express any viewpoint, and choose leaders through multiparty elections.

The Soviet Union, on the other hand, embraced a communist ideology that stressed equality and cooperation among all citizens. In the Soviet socialist system, the state owned all businesses and had tight control over the economy. An authoritarian, one-party government censored the press and otherwise squashed criticism of its activities.

▲ At the age of forty-three, John F. Kennedy became the youngest elected U.S. president in history. The Cuban missile crisis would be the hardest test of his life.

KENNEDY AND KHRUSHCHEV

Both Kennedy and Khrushchev had personal reasons for believing strongly in their own political systems. Kennedy was the son of a millionaire. His father, Joseph Kennedy, became wealthy through stock market investments and then went into politics, serving as ambassador to Britain in the 1930s. He encouraged his sons to be ambitious and competitive and used his vast fortune to fund their political careers.

Khrushchev, the son of a peasant, could barely read until he was in his twenties. Through hard work and political skill, he rose through the ranks of the Communist Party. While Khrushchev might have been ruthless, he was also an idealist, certain that communism was the best possible political system and would one day triumph around the world.

The Soviet premier never forgot his poor background. "I went about barefoot and in rags," he told Western diplomats. "When you were in the nursery I was herding cows for two kopeks." To Khrushchev, capitalist freedom was "the freedom to exploit, the freedom to rob, the freedom to die of starvation."

▽ Nikita Khrushchev believed that the Soviet Union could overtake the West and show the way forward for all humankind. Addressing the United States, he boasted, "We will bury you!"

DIFFERENT VIEWS

In his memoirs, Khrushchev describes his vision of the communist future:

"Progress is on our side and victory will inevitably be ours … We Communists believe that Capitalism is a hell in which laboring people are condemned to slavery. We are building Socialism … Our way of life is paradise for mankind."

KHRUSHCHEV REMEMBERS BY NIKITA KHRUSHCHEV

Kennedy saw communism very differently:

"The enemy is the Communist system itself — implacable, insatiable, unceasing in its drive for world domination … It is … a struggle for supremacy between two conflicting ideologies: freedom under God versus ruthless, godless tyranny."

KENNEDY IN A SPEECH IN SEPTEMBER 1960, QUOTED IN KENNEDY V. KHRUSHCHEV, THE CRISIS YEARS BY MICHAEL R. BESCHLOSS

THE NUCLEAR ARMS RACE

On August 6, 1945, the United States dropped the world's first
atomic bomb on the Japanese city of Hiroshima, immediately
destroying the city and killing 80,000 people. Three days later,
it dropped a second atomic bomb on Nagasaki, destroying that
city as well and killing 75,000 more people. Japan then
surrendered, ending World War II. President Harry Truman,
who had ordered the bombings, declared that this new weapon
was "the greatest thing in history."

The United States had unleashed a weapon with the
potential to end human civilization, and the cities of Hiroshima
and Nagasaki were proof that it was prepared to use this
weapon. The Soviets reacted by building their own atomic
bomb, which they successfully tested in September 1949.

In response, the United States developed the hydrogen
bomb, a nuclear weapon that was a thousand times more
powerful than the atomic bomb. When the hydrogen bomb
was first tested, in November 1952, it destroyed an entire
Pacific island. Nine months later, the Soviets also successfully
detonated a hydrogen bomb.

MISSILES

Unlike the large, heavy atomic bomb, which had to be carried
in a plane, the hydrogen bomb was small and light and could
be carried on a missile. In the United States, the world's best

missile scientists — Germans who had designed rockets for Hitler during World War II — began developing missiles that could carry hydrogen bombs over great distances. By 1957, they had produced the Atlas missile, which could travel over 6,000 miles (9,655 kilometers) and land within 1 mile (1.6 km) of its target. The Atlas was the world's first intercontinental ballistic missile (ICBM).

NUCLEAR DETERRENCE

Because nuclear weapons had such incredible destructive power, the United States and the Soviet Union were forced to rethink their use. Neither side could afford to drop hydrogen bombs on the other, because its own losses would be too great. The United States and the Soviet Union kept building nuclear weapons, however, in order to deter the other side from using its nuclear arsenal.

MILITARY-INDUSTRIAL COMPLEX

The perceived threat from the Soviet Union was not the only reason that the United States continued building nuclear weapons. During World War II, a huge weapons industry came into existence, employing three and a half million men and women. After the war, this industry found a new role building missiles and other military equipment.

The U.S. military and the weapons industry formed an influential partnership that U.S. president Dwight Eisenhower called the "military-industrial complex."

"UNWARRANTED INFLUENCE"

In his last speech as president in January 1961, Dwight Eisenhower warned against the influence of the "military-industrial complex":

"This conjunction of an immense military establishment and a large arms industry is new in the American experience. The total influence — economic, political, even spiritual — is felt in every city, every State house, every office of the Federal government ... In the councils of government, we must guard against the acquisition of unwarranted influence, whether sought or unsought, by the military-industrial complex."

PUBLIC PAPERS OF THE PRESIDENTS

▼ President Harry Truman ordered the dropping of atomic bombs in Japan to end the war and save the lives of American soldiers. He started the nuclear arms race, however, which would eventually threaten the entire world.

KHRUSHCHEV'S BLUFF

On October 4, 1957, the Soviet Union launched a rocket carrying *Sputnik*, the world's first space satellite. This launch stunned the United States, which took it as evidence that the Soviets were now able to build long-range missiles.

Khrushchev was happy to let the United States believe in Soviet long-range missiles. In late 1959, he even claimed that his missiles could "hit a fly in space." He also said that Soviet factories were turning out ICBMs "like sausages."

In fact, Khrushchev was bluffing. Soviet scientists might have been able to send a rocket into space, but they could not match the accuracy of American ICBMs. During test flights, Soviet ICBMs often flew wildly off course. The Soviets could only build effective short-range missiles, which could target western Europe but could not reach the United States.

Khrushchev did not want to spend more money on the military. His first goal was to raise Soviet living standards and rebuild the economy, which had been shattered by World War II. The Soviet leader welcomed nuclear weapons because they were potentially cheaper than conventional forces, but he did not want to build vast numbers of them. He hoped that his nuclear bluff would be a substitute for actual weapons.

THE "MISSILE GAP"

Khrushchev's bluff convinced many Americans that there was a "missile gap" between the United States and the Soviet Union. When Kennedy campaigned for the U.S. presidency in 1960, he promised to close this gap and put the United States back in the lead.

Once he became president, Kennedy learned from the military that the United States was the true leader in the arms race. Photographs taken by spy planes showed that the Soviet Union had very few ICBMs.

U.S. AND SOVIET STRATEGIC WARHEADS

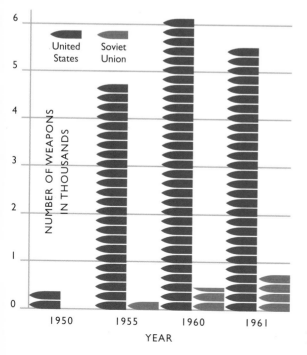

United States

Soviet Union

NUMBER OF WEAPONS IN THOUSANDS

6

5

4

3

2

1

0

1950   1955   1960   1961

YEAR

10

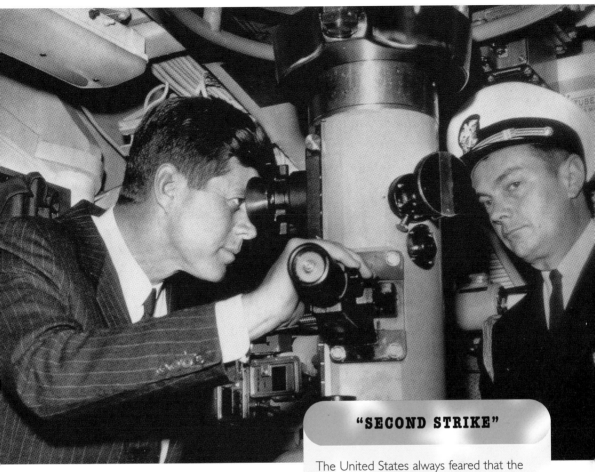

▲ In April 1962, President Kennedy looks through the periscope of a new Polaris submarine.

Kennedy still went ahead with his nuclear buildup. By 1961, the United States possessed 18,000 nuclear weapons with a million times the destructive power of the bomb dropped on Hiroshima. The U.S. lead in nuclear weapons had now reached seventeen-to-one against the Soviet Union.

In October 1961, Kennedy called Khrushchev's bluff by announcing to the world just how far behind the Soviets were to the United States.

"SECOND STRIKE"

The United States always feared that the Soviet Union might consider a nuclear war winnable if it could deliver a "first strike" that would prevent U.S. retaliation. To deter such an attack, the United States developed "second-strike" capability — it would survive a first strike and hit back. "Second-strike" readiness became the justification for building thousands of nuclear weapons.

The Polaris submarine was the perfect "second-strike" weapon. Developed in 1960, the Polaris carried nuclear missiles. Even if all land-based U.S. missile sites were knocked out in a surprise attack, Polaris submarines would still be able to devastate the Soviet Union.

CHAPTER THREE

Revolutionary Cuba

Because of Cuba's size — it is the largest island in the Caribbean — and its closeness to the U.S. coast, it has always been of special interest to the United States. Direct U.S. involvement began in the late 1890s, after Cubans rebelled against their Spanish rulers and the United States stepped in on behalf of Cuban independence.

During the Spanish-American War of 1898, the United States quickly defeated the Spaniards, who gave up control of Cuba. With the war over, however, U.S. support for Cuban independence seemed less certain. Cubans were not invited to peace talks with the Spaniards, and U.S. troops occupied Cuba for the next four years.

In 1902 the island was at last granted independence, but on terms favorable to the United States. Under the new Cuban constitution, the United States had the right to intervene in

▼ The Texaco oil refinery at Santiago de Cuba. Texaco was one of many U.S. businesses that invested heavily in Cuba.

Cuban affairs whenever it felt its interests were threatened. Cuba also had to accept the presence of a large U.S. military base at Guantanamo Bay. A series of corrupt leaders governed the island.

Fulgencio Batista began dominating Cuba in 1933. At first, Batista ruled behind the scenes, controlling five consecutive Cuban presidents. In 1952, however, when it appeared that a rival might win the presidential election, he staged a coup and made himself dictator. By demanding bribes and protection money, Batista amassed a personal fortune worth $300 million.

HAVANA

Under Batista, the Cuban capital city of Havana became a favorite destination for American tourists, who came for the city's gambling and nightlife. Several luxury hotels and casinos were built along Havana's waterfront, but behind this facade lay a city of slums, with about 5,000 beggars.

PEASANTS

In the countryside, the majority of Cuban peasants also lived in poverty. Their main source of work, cutting sugarcane, was seasonal, so for six months of the year they might be unemployed. The peasants lived in wooden huts without running water, toilets, or electricity. They had few schools and almost no doctors. It was said that Cuba was a land where only cattle were vaccinated.

▲ In the 1950s, Cuban dictator Fulgencio Batista's open corruption and brutal treatment of political opponents made him increasingly unpopular with the Cuban people.

U.S. BUSINESS IN CUBA

Following Cuban independence, U.S. businesses invested heavily in the island. By the 1950s, U.S. companies controlled 90% of Cuba's mines and cattle ranches, almost 100% of its oil-refining industry, 50% of its railways, and 40% of its sugar industry. Almost all consumer goods in Cuban shops were imported from the United States.

FIDEL CASTRO

In December 1956, a group of eighty-one revolutionaries sailed from Mexico, where they had been training, to the island of Cuba. Their leader was a thirty-one-year-old Cuban lawyer named Fidel Castro.

Castro's men found safety in the mountains of the Sierra Maestra, which became their base for a guerrilla campaign against the Batista regime that lasted for three years. Castro

▼ In 1957, a U.S. journalist took this photograph of Fidel Castro in his mountain hideout. The young bearded guerrilla leader fascinated many American newspaper readers, who did not know what to make of him.

promised to restore democracy and freedom, and he won the support of a broad range of Cubans. By the end of the campaign, Batista had become so unpopular that even the United States no longer supported him. On New Year's Day, 1959, he fled the country, and Castro entered Havana in triumph.

Despite his leftist ideas, in 1959 Castro did not consider himself a communist. Instead, he saw himself as a nationalist whose main goal was giving the Cuban people back their independence and self-respect. He promised to end Cuba's reliance on the United States and to introduce sweeping social reforms.

SOVIET TRADE

Alexander Alexeyev, a Russian journalist in Cuba, acted as a go-between for Castro and Khrushchev:

"Fidel … asked if we could buy some of his sugar — at least a symbolic quantity … When I handed [Khrushchev's reply] to Fidel, it said that we, the Soviet Union, were ready to buy all the sugar, those 700,000 tons rejected by the Americans. And not only that year's consignment but also the next year's. That was really an event! I was at the rally. There were one million people there. I could see for myself the joy of the Cuban people. They were throwing their berets in the air."

ALEXANDER ALEXEYEV QUOTED IN *KENNEDY V. KHRUSHCHEV, THE CRISIS YEARS* BY MICHAEL R. BESCHLOSS

U.S. CONFLICT

One of Castro's first acts was to break up large agricultural landholdings — most of which were owned by U.S. businesses — and redistribute the land among small peasant cooperatives.

The United States reacted to the land seizure by reducing the amount of sugar it bought from Cuba, but Castro responded by seizing more American-owned property. President Eisenhower then banned all Cuban sugar imports. Castro warned that the ban would "cost Americans in Cuba down to the nails in their shoes."

SOVIET CREDITS

Castro was desperate to find other trading partners for Cuba. He approached the Soviet Union, which agreed to buy all the sugar Cuba produced. In exchange for the sugar, Khrushchev offered Castro credits to buy Soviet machinery and oil. When U.S. refineries in Cuba refused to refine Soviet oil, Castro "nationalized" them, making them the property of the new Cuban state.

▲ Castro promised a
better future for the
children of Cuba.

THE NEW CUBA

In addition to redistributing large landholdings, Castro took
other measures that radically changed Cuban life.

To address Cuba's housing problem, Castro cut all rents in
half and banned the ownership of second homes. He then
ordered rent payments be converted into mortgages, turning
a half-million Cuban tenants into home owners.

In the countryside, Castro ordered the construction of
hundreds of medical centers, which provided free health care
to all, and he also launched a campaign against illiteracy. In
1961, Cuban schools were shut down for eight months so that
100,000 teachers and students could travel to the countryside
and teach Cuban peasants to read and write.

A DIVIDED NATION

Castro's measures divided the Cuban people. Many middle-class Cubans had initially supported Castro, but they felt betrayed by him when he refused to hold elections or allow a free press. They were also hit hard by Castro's economic reforms, losing jobs provided by American businesses as well as income from rents. Thousands of these middle-class Cubans fled to the United States, where they denounced Castro as a communist dictator.

Yet Castro had massive support from Cuba's poor citizens, who for the first time in their lives were being provided with decent homes, health care, and education. Before the revolution, black and mixed-race Cubans had been considered second-class citizens, and one of Castro's first acts as the new Cuban leader was to open the island's white-only beaches to all Cubans. Castro seemed to be breaking down the island's old class and race barriers, and he was inciting a new sense of solidarity and pride among many Cuban people.

The popularity of the new regime was also shown by the thousands of ordinary Cubans who joined the people's militia. These were unprofessional, part-time soldiers who kept their guns at home but were ready to defend the revolution at Fidel's call. A hated dictator could never allow so many citizens to own weapons.

Regardless of his faults, Castro was definitely a new kind of Cuban leader. Unlike Batista, he did not seem bent on making himself rich. He lived simply and was often photographed cutting sugar-cane alongside workers in the fields, to show that he was a man of the people, working to improve Cubans' lives.

CASTRO'S CHARISMA

Everyone who met Castro was struck by his ability to attract and inspire followers. Even anti-communist hard-liner Richard Nixon remarked on this charisma:

"Castro was one of the most striking foreign officials I met during my eight years as vice president. He seemed to have that indefinable quality which, for good or evil, makes a leader of men. He had a compelling intense voice, sparkling black eyes, and he radiated vitality."

FROM *THE BRINK: CUBA, CASTRO AND JOHN F. KENNEDY,* 1964
BY DAVID DETZER

In Cuba, Russian journalist Alexander Alexeyev was impressed by the hero worship Castro inspired:

"I found that at least ninety per cent of the people were for Fidel … They idolized him … Every Cuban house had graffiti saying, 'Fidel, this is your home!'"

ALEXANDER ALEXEYEV QUOTED IN *KENNEDY V. KHRUSHCHEV,*
THE CRISIS YEARS BY MICHAEL R. BESCHLOSS

BAY OF PIGS

After Kennedy became U.S. president in January 1961, he learned that plans were already in place to overthrow Fidel Castro with an invasion army of 1,500 Cuban émigrés. For months, the Central Intelligence Agency, or CIA, had been training the émigrés in bases in Guatemala.

Allan Dulles, the head of the CIA, told Kennedy that the invasion had an excellent chance for success. Dulles and Kennedy both believed that Castro was deeply unpopular in Cuba. Once the invasion took place, Dulles promised, there would be a general uprising against Castro. Dulles also pointed out that Kennedy could deny any involvement in the operation. The president approved the plan, on the condition that no U.S. troops be used.

FIASCO

The invasion of Cuba began on April 14, 1962. It was a disastrous failure. The CIA had chosen the worst possible place to invade; the Cuban émigrés found themselves trapped on their beachhead at the Bay of Pigs on the south coast of Cuba, hemmed in by swamps. The invaders were outgunned and easily defeated by troops led personally by Castro.

As the scale of the defeat became clear, Admiral Burke of the U.S. Navy begged Kennedy to provide air support for the invasion. The President refused. "I don't want the United States involved with this," Kennedy explained. Admiral Burke reportedly replied, "Hell, Mr. President, we are involved!"

The Cuban people did not, as predicted, rise up against Castro. Instead, thousands of Cubans came forward to defend their homeland against the invaders. Even Cubans who had opposed Castro now saw him as a patriotic hero.

THE CIA

The Central Intelligence Agency, or CIA, was established in 1947 to gather foreign intelligence in order to protect U.S. security. The CIA later specialized in covert, or secret, operations — acts that could be denied by the government. One of the agency's greatest successes came in 1954, when it organized a coup against Guatemalan president Jacobo Arbenz. Like Castro, Arbenz antagonized U.S. business. In particular, he tried to nationalize lands held by the powerful United Fruit Company.

AFTERMATH

Following the Bay of Pigs fiasco, Castro's regime became stronger than ever. Castro was now even more hostile towards the United States, and in December 1961 he declared himself a communist.

The new president of the United States had been humiliated. Kennedy bitterly reproached himself for having listened to the military experts. "All my life I've known better than to depend on the experts," he said. "How could I have been so stupid, to let them go ahead?"

▲ Cuban émigrés, captured during the disastrous Bay of Pigs invasion, are marched to prison.

CALL TO ARMS

On February 4, 1962, Castro called on the poor of Latin America to stage their own revolutions:

"Now history will have to take the poor of America into account, the exploited and spurned of Latin America … And the wave of anger, of demands for justice, of claims for rights, which is beginning to sweep Latin America will not stop."

FIDEL CASTRO SPEAKS EDITED BY MARTIN KENNER
AND JAMES PETRAS

CHAPTER FOUR

Cold Warfare

A month after the Bay of Pigs, Kennedy traveled to Vienna, Austria, to meet Khrushchev. While Kennedy was still stinging from the Bay of Pigs fiasco, the Soviet premier was in a confident mood; he was enjoying a public relations triumph. On April 12, 1961, the Soviet Union had sent the first man into space, cosmonaut Yuri Gagarin.

Cuba was only briefly discussed. Khrushchev insisted that Cuba was not a threat to the United States. He also told Kennedy that Castro was not even a communist, but "you are well on the way to making him a good one."

◄ After his space flight, Yuri Gagarin became an international hero. Upon his return to Earth, his first words to Khrushchev were, "Now let the other countries try to catch us."

BERLIN

The most important issue in Vienna was the question of Berlin, which at the time seemed a much more troublesome spot than Cuba. Although Berlin was located in the heart of communist East Germany, the communists only controlled the eastern part of the city. In Kennedy's words, West Berlin was "an island of freedom in a communist sea." It survived thanks to its occupying force of U.S., French, and British troops. This occupation had continued because, technically, World War II had not formally ended. A peace treaty to settle the status of Germany had never been signed.

DIVIDED GERMANY

After World War II, the Soviet Union and the United States disagreed on the future of Germany. U.S. plans called for a united, democratic Germany with Berlin as its capital. The Soviets, who lost twenty million people from Hitler's assaults, wanted to keep Germany divided. In East Germany, they established the communist German Democratic Republic (GDR), which the United States refused to recognize. West Germany became the democratic Federal Republic of Germany (FRG).

KHRUSHCHEV'S DEMANDS

For Khrushchev, Berlin represented a serious problem. Every week, about 10,000 East Germans used Berlin as an escape route to the West. For the most part, those escaping were East Germany's best-educated people. They knew they could earn much more money in West Germany, where there was an economic boom. This drain of talent was threatening to ruin the already weak East German economy.

In Vienna, Khrushchev demanded that Kennedy sign a peace treaty recognizing East Germany and giving it control over West Berlin. If Kennedy refused, Khrushchev insisted, in six months the Soviets would sign their own peace treaty with the East Germans.

Trying to intimidate Kennedy, Khrushchev smashed a table with his hand and cried, "I want peace. But if you want war, that is your problem." Kennedy replied, "It is you, not I, who wants to force a change."

▼ Kennedy greets Khrushchev in Vienna. The smiles on their faces quickly vanished once the talks began.

▲ East German workers build the wall that will separate the two halves of Berlin for the next twenty-eight years.

THE BERLIN WALL

At midnight on August 12, 1961, East German workers began building a barrier along the border between East and West Berlin. Meant to seal off communist-controlled East Berlin from the West, the barrier was at first made of barbed wire but was soon replaced by a concrete wall.

The building of the wall caused widespread alarm in West Berlin, where it was seen as the first step in a Soviet takeover. Few people thought that the wall would be permanent. Khrushchev's threat to seize West Berlin in December still stood.

To reaffirm his commitment to defend West Berlin, Kennedy sent 1,500 U.S. troops to the city. They were vastly outnumbered by Soviet troops, but the president's gesture helped keep up the West Berliners' morale.

WALL OR WAR?

Although he would not say so publicly, Kennedy believed that the wall was a possible solution to the Berlin crisis:

"Why would Khrushchev put up a wall if he really intended to seize West Berlin? There wouldn't be any need of a wall if he occupied the whole city. This is his way out of his predicament. It's not a very nice solution, but a wall is a hell of a lot better than a war."

KENNEDY V. KHRUSHCHEV, THE CRISIS YEARS BY MICHAEL R. BESCHLOSS

Tensions between the Soviet Union and the United States over Berlin remained high through the end of 1961. Yet Khrushchev allowed his December deadline to pass without signing a treaty with the East Germans, and the Berlin crisis faded from the news. Kennedy, however, worried about Berlin for the rest of his presidency. At any moment, he believed, Khrushchev could seize the city and spark a new crisis.

Although the Berlin Wall ended the problem of East Germans fleeing to the West, it was not a victory for Khrushchev. The Soviet premier insisted that the wall was built "to guard the gates of the Socialist paradise," but it was obviously meant to imprison the East Germans. Its existence undermined the legitimacy of the East German state.

In 1961, few people could have guessed that the Berlin Wall would stand for the next 28 years, separating families and friends. With its tall watchtowers — manned by guards with machine guns and dogs — it stood as a powerful symbol of communist tyranny.

▼ In August 1961, a U.S. tank makes a show of force on a Berlin street.

STIRRING THINGS UP

Robert Kennedy described the aim of Operation Mongoose in an internal memo:

"My idea is to stir things up on the island with espionage, sabotage, general disorder, run and operated by the Cubans themselves … Do not know if we will be successful in overthrowing Castro but we have nothing to lose …"

ROBERT KENNEDY AND HIS TIMES BY ARTHUR M. SCHLESINGER JR.

THE SECRET WAR

While the Berlin crisis filled the newspapers, another, secret phase of the Cold War began. In November 1961, Kennedy authorized a new plan, called "Operation Mongoose," to strike at Fidel Castro's hold on Cuba.

The plan called for undermining Castro's regime through sabotage and even assassination. It was supervised by the president's younger brother, U.S. attorney general Robert F. Kennedy. Bobby was the president's closest adviser and the one man he trusted completely. After the Bay of Pigs, both brothers felt a personal animosity towards Castro, and they were determined to overthrow him.

Bobby Kennedy took his plan to the heads of the CIA, who welcomed the chance to restore the agency's reputation after the Bay of Pigs fiasco. With a $50 million budget, they set up a huge operations center in Miami, Florida, that employed 400 U.S. agents and 2,000 Cuban émigrés. In the first seven months of 1962, the Operation Mongoose team carried out roughly 6,000 acts in Cuba, including blowing up bridges and factories and burning down fields of sugarcane.

◀ Bobby Kennedy (on right) was fiercely loyal to his older brother, and he was ruthless with anyone whom he saw as a threat to the president.

The United States also let it be known that U.S. marines would stage large-scale exercises in the Caribbean in October 1962. The soldiers would practice invading an island to overthrow an imaginary dictator named "Ortsac" — Castro spelled backwards.

Fidel Castro was certain that the United States planned to invade Cuba. This belief was reinforced by his own agents in Florida, who reported talk among Cuban émigrés about a new invasion that would accomplish what the Bay of Pigs had not.

Despite U.S. actions towards Cuba, Kennedy had not intended to invade the island. Castro, however, was convinced that a real invasion was about to take place, and he passed this alarming news on to Moscow.

▲ El Encanto, one of Havana's biggest department stores, lies in ruins. It had been burned down by Cuban émigrés trained and armed by the CIA.

CIA PLOTS

The CIA hatched many schemes to kill or discredit Castro, including the following:
- Send Castro a present of a scuba diving suit impregnated with deadly bacteria (Castro was an enthusiastic diver).
- Give Castro a cigar soaked with the drug LSD, so he would speak gibberish during one of his talks to the Cuban people.
- Dose Castro with a powder that would make his beard fall out, thus robbing him of his charisma.
- Distribute fake photographs showing *"an obese Castro with two beauties … ostensibly within a room in the Castro residence, lavishly furnished and a table briming [sic] over with the most delectable Cuban food with an underlying caption … such as 'My ration is different.'"*

FROM OPERATION MONGOOSE DOCUMENT

CHAPTER FIVE

Khrushchev's Missile Gamble

Castro convinced Khrushchev that the United States was about to invade Cuba. The Soviet premier believed he had to do something to protect the only communist state in the West. At some point in the spring of 1962, he decided to install nuclear missiles in Cuba.

STRATEGIC BALANCE

Cuban defense was not Khrushchev's only motive for installing the missiles. The previous September, Kennedy humiliated Khrushchev by announcing that the United States

▼ Castro and Khrushchev. While Castro needed Soviet weapons and trade, Khrushchev needed Castro's example as the popular and charismatic leader of a communist country in the Western hemisphere.

actually possessed far more missiles than the Soviet Union, despite Khrushchev's claims to the contrary. Khrushchev was now under great pressure from the Soviet military to increase spending on long-range and submarine-launched nuclear missiles that could reach the United States. Yet Khrushchev wanted to cut the military budget, not increase it. Military spending undermined his central political aim, which was to raise the living standards of Soviet citizens.

While the Soviet Union had few long-range missiles, it did have short-range missiles that could hit the United States from Cuba. Khrushchev saw a cheap and easy way to undercut U.S. superiority.

PROTECTING CUBA

In his memoirs, Khrushchev explained the importance of protecting Cuba:

"We had an obligation to do everything in our power to protect Cuba's existence as a Socialist country and as a working example to the other countries of Latin America … One thought kept hammering at my brain: what will happen if we lose Cuba? I knew it would be a terrible blow to Marxism-Leninism. It would gravely diminish our stature throughout the world, but especially in Latin America."

KHRUSHCHEV REMEMBERS BY NIKITA KHRUSHCHEV

PRESTIGE

Khrushchev also knew that Soviet missiles in Cuba would boost his country's prestige. In 1962 Khrushchev had fallen out with Mao Tse-tung, the ruler of communist China. Mao had accused Khrushchev of weakness in failing to drive the United States out of West Berlin. He challenged the Soviet Union's status as the world leader of communism.

From his dealings with the United States, Khrushchev had concluded that the United States considered the Soviet Union to be a second-class nation rather than a superpower. He bitterly resented the U.S. installation of missiles in Turkey, close to the Soviet border. Khrushchev later wrote that, by sending missiles to Cuba, he "would be doing nothing more than giving them [Americans] a bit of their own medicine."

Despite all the potential benefits of Soviet missiles in Cuba, however, installing them would still be a huge gamble. Khrushchev had no idea how the United States would react to the presence of Soviet nuclear missiles on the island.

▲ In October 1962, a Soviet cargo ship loaded with missiles steams towards Cuba.

SECRET INSTALLATION

Khrushchev decided that the only way to install missiles in Cuba was to do so secretly. He believed that if he announced his plan in advance the United States would be certain to take action. He might then have to back down.

Secret installation, however, had its disadvantages. First, the installation might be detected. Second, it took away the leverage of world opinion. If the Soviets acted openly, the United States would have difficulty rallying the world to its cause, since Khrushchev could argue that the Soviets were doing what the United States had already done in Turkey.

In the summer of 1962, the number of Soviet ships traveling to Cuba rose dramatically. Thirty cargo ships sailed in July, followed by thirty-seven in August, and sixty-six in September. The Soviets claimed the ships were only carrying tools and farm machinery.

CASTRO'S DOUBTS

Fidel Castro welcomed Khrushchev's offer of nuclear missiles, but he believed that secret installation was a mistake:

"We were within our most absolute right to do so [install them]. And why, if we had the right, were we going to act in a way that made it seem that we were doing something wrong?"

INTERVIEWED IN BBC-TV PROGRAM *EYEBALL TO EYEBALL* (1992)

The cargo ships were not, of course, carrying farm machinery. Instead, the ships delivered to Cuba 162 nuclear warheads and missiles, 42 jet bombers capable of carrying nuclear weapons, 150 jet fighter planes, 350 tanks, and 700 anti-aircraft guns.

Passenger ships carrying 42,000 Soviet troops and technicians also traveled to Cuba that summer. The first arrivals were dressed as tourists in khaki shorts and white short-sleeved shirts. They aroused the suspicion of U.S. observers, who noticed that they wore only two types of shirt and formed in disciplined ranks on the dockside before moving out in truck convoys.

The construction of the missile bases was a huge operation. New roads had to be built for the trucks carrying the missiles, and large areas of jungle had to be cleared for launchpads and storage buildings. The Soviets would have great difficulty keeping U.S. spy planes from detecting so much activity.

SOVIET MISSILES IN CUBA

STRATEGIC WEAPONS
(Targeted U.S. cities)
SS-4. A medium-range ballistic missile (MRBM) that was fired from a mobile launcher and had a range of 1,060 miles (1,700 km).
SS-5. An intermediate-range ballistic missile (IRBM), that fired from a special launchpad and had a range of 2,240 miles (3, 600 km).

TACTICAL WEAPONS
(Short-range, for use in battle)
FROG-7. This "free-rocket-over-ground" missile was unguided and had a range of 25 miles (40 km).
Cruise missile. A slow-flying pilotless plane.

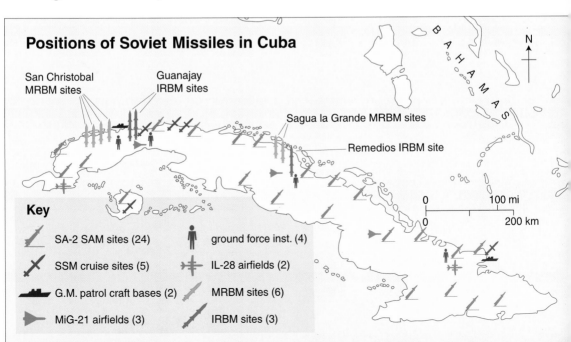

Positions of Soviet Missiles in Cuba

San Christobal MRBM sites

Guanajay IRBM sites

Sagua la Grande MRBM sites

Remedios IRBM site

Key

- SA-2 SAM sites (24)
- SSM cruise sites (5)
- G.M. patrol craft bases (2)
- MiG-21 airfields (3)
- ground force inst. (4)
- IL-28 airfields (2)
- MRBM sites (6)
- IRBM sites (3)

0   100 mi
0   200 km

CHAPTER SIX

Reacting to the Missiles

▲ A photograph of the Soviet missile sites at San Christobal, Cuba, taken by a U-2 spy plane on October 25, 1962.

SOVIET ASSURANCES

In his memoir of the missile crisis, Robert Kennedy describes meeting Soviet ambassador Anatoly Dobrynin on September 4, 1962:

"He said that I could assure the President that this military buildup was not of any significance and that Khrushchev would do nothing to disrupt the relationship of our two countries during this period prior to the election. Chairman Khrushchev, he said, liked President Kennedy and did not wish to embarrass him."

THIRTEEN DAYS BY ROBERT F. KENNEDY

In September 1962, Democrats and Republicans were competing for control of Congress, which would be decided in the upcoming November elections. Nuclear missiles had not yet been discovered in Cuba, but increased Soviet activity there had become an election issue. Republicans accused Kennedy, a Democrat, of doing nothing while the Soviets turned Cuba into a military base.

Worried about the Soviet military buildup, Kennedy announced that he would not tolerate any offensive weapons being sent to Cuba. Khrushchev assured him that the only weapons going to the island were defensive.

▼ Khrushchev had little chance of keeping his missiles secret from U.S. U-2 planes, which made regular flights over Cuba.

PHOTOGRAPHS

On Sunday, October 14, a U-2 spy plane piloted by Major Rudolf Anderson took aeriel photographs of western Cuba. The following day, the photos were blown up and analyzed by experts at the CIA's Photographic Interpretation Center. Their attention was immediately drawn to several oblong objects, which they recognized as canvas-covered missiles sitting on trailers. They concluded that they were looking at SS-4s, which were Soviet medium-range ballistic missiles. With a range of 1,060 miles (1,700 km), these missiles could strike at both New York City and Washington, D.C.

At 8:45 a.m. on October 16, presidential national security adviser McGeorge Bundy broke the news to Kennedy, who was still in his bathrobe. Kennedy's first reaction was one of fury that Khrushchev had lied to him. The president is said to have exclaimed, "He can't do this to me!"

Kennedy was baffled by the discovery. He could not understand Khrushchev's motivation. Khrushchev had never placed any nuclear weapons outside the Soviet Union. Why would he now be willing to risk a war over Cuba?

Mutual misunderstanding and incomprehension would be a major problem throughout the coming crisis.

THE U-2

Designed in 1955, the U-2 spy plane could fly at an altitude of 13 miles (21 km). The U-2 took off almost vertically and flew at 460 miles (740 km) an hour. Its purpose was to take photographs unobserved and out of the reach of anti-aircraft guns, and it carried seven cameras with amazingly sophisticated lenses. In 1955, the Air Force published photographs of a golf course taken by a U-2 from a height of more than 9 miles (14.5 km). The photos clearly showed golf balls lying in the grass.

31

IN THE WHITE HOUSE

By 11:45 a.m., the president had assembled his chief advisers in the White House to discuss the situation. For the next twelve days, these advisers met continuously. The group would later be known as Ex-Comm, which is short for "Executive Committee of the National Security Council."

Kennedy blamed the Bay of Pigs disaster on his failure to listen to a wide range of opinions. Now he encouraged a completely open discussion, with all viewpoints given equal weight. To encourage honesty, the president even decided not to attend all the meetings, so that the advisers would not simply say what they thought he wanted to hear.

The advisers met in secret for the first five days of the crisis, pretending to the outside world that nothing was wrong. On October 18, Kennedy saw Andrei Gromyko, the Soviet foreign minister. When Gromyko repeated Khrushchev's assurance that the Soviets would never send offensive weapons to Cuba, Kennedy had to hide his anger.

▲ President Kennedy listens thoughtfully to his Ex-Comm advisers.

EX-COMM

There were twenty members of Ex-Comm, though eight members only attended occasional meetings. The most important members were:

Robert McNamara, Secretary of Defense
Paul Nitze, Assistant Secretary of Defense
Dean Rusk, Secretary of State
George Ball, Under Secretary of State
Roswell Gilpatric, Under Secretary of State
Douglas Dillon, Secretary of the Treasury
John McCone, Director of the CIA
General Maxwell Taylor, Chairman of the Joint
  Chiefs of Staff
Theodore Sorensen, the President's chief adviser
  and speech writer
Llewellyn Thompson, Adviser on Soviet affairs
McGeorge Bundy, Special Assistant for National
  Security Affairs
Robert F. Kennedy, U.S. Attorney General

While the Ex-Comm members might not have agreed on the best strategy for handling the crisis, they did agree that the president had to get the missiles removed from Cuba. Kennedy could not allow Castro to threaten the United States with nuclear weapons.

The Ex-Comm members could only offer advice. In the end, the final decision rested with the president alone. Gazing out of the window, President Kennedy is reported to have said, "I guess I'd better earn my salary this week."

▲ President Kennedy meets with Soviet foreign minister Gromyko and ambassador Dobrynin. On the surface, the meeting was friendly. Kennedy, however, now knew about the missiles and was secretly furious.

PRESSURE

In his memoir of the missile crisis, Robert Kennedy describes the awesome sense of responsibility felt by the members of Ex-Comm:

"Each one of us was being asked to make a recommendation which, if wrong and if accepted, could mean the destruction of the human race."

THIRTEEN DAYS BY ROBERT F. KENNEDY

HOW DO WE STOP?

Secretary of Defense Robert McNamara was opposed to a surprise attack against Cuba:

"I don't know quite what kind of a world we live in after we've struck Cuba, and we, we've started it ... How, how do we stop at that point?"

THE KENNEDY TAPES: INSIDE THE WHITE HOUSE DURING THE CUBAN MISSILE CRISIS EDITED BY E. R. MAY AND P. D. ZELIKOW

OPTIONS

While Ex-Comm met in the White House to discuss Kennedy's options, the U.S. military's Joint Chiefs of Staff met in the Pentagon. Their attitude towards the crisis was best expressed by the Air Force chief, General Curtis LeMay, who at one point said, "Bomb the hell out of them!"

The chiefs recommended a large-scale surprise attack on the missile sites. General Maxwell Taylor, Chairman of the Joint Chiefs of Staff, pointed out that if the Soviets received any warning they could hide the missiles in the Cuban jungle. A surprise attack would also eliminate the threat of retaliation from the Cuban missiles.

Kennedy asked the chiefs what they thought the Soviet response would be to a U.S. attack on Cuba. General LeMay assured Kennedy that the Soviets would do nothing, but the president was skeptical. He reportedly said, "If they don't take action in Cuba, they certainly will in Berlin."

DOUBTS

As the debate continued, members of Ex-Comm began to have growing doubts about a surprise attack. Robert Kennedy

◀ General Curtis LeMay headed the U.S. Air Force and was perhaps the most aggressive "hawk" in the military. LeMay strongly advocated for bombing Cuba.

and Robert McNamara argued against such an attack. They recalled the outrage of the American people when Japan bombed Pearl Harbor in a surprise raid. Japanese general Tojo had been hanged as a war criminal for the attack. How could the United States now adopt the same tactic?

THE BLOCKADE OPTION

McNamara suggested a naval blockade on Cuba. The United States would stop and search all Soviet ships heading for the island and turn back any carrying weapons. A blockade had the advantage of putting limited pressure on the Soviets while still giving them the chance to back down. If the blockade failed, pressure on the Soviets could be increased in other ways. The United States could still attack Cuba, but only if the blockade failed.

THE MORAL POSITION

Robert Kennedy was opposed to a surprise attack against Cuba:

"Like others, I could not accept the idea that the United States would rain bombs on Cuba, killing thousands and thousands of civilians in a surprise attack ... They were ... advocating a surprise attack by a very large nation against a very small one. This, I said, could not be undertaken if we were to maintain our moral position at home and around the globe. Our struggle against Communism throughout the world was far more than physical survival."

THIRTEEN DAYS BY ROBERT F. KENNEDY

▼ Secretary of Defense Robert McNamara speaks to the press in August 1961, at the height of the crisis over the Berlin Wall.

THE MILITARY VIEW

U.S. general Maxwell Taylor was strongly against the blockade option:

"Khrushchev could simply bring his ships just short of the quarantine line and stand there and scream to the world over the violation of international law we were indulging in, and meanwhile start that argument going while his missiles completed their readiness in the island."

ON THE BRINK: AMERICANS AND SOVIETS RE-EXAMINE THE CUBAN MISSILE CRISIS BY JAMES G. BLIGHT AND DAVID WELCH

THE PRESIDENT DECIDES

On Saturday, October 20, Kennedy announced his decision to Ex-Comm. He would impose a naval blockade on Cuba before he launched an air strike.

General Taylor argued against this decision. He pointed out that a blockade would not force the removal of weapons already in Cuba, so military action would still be necessary to rid the island of those weapons. A blockade would simply give the Soviets time to finish preparing their existing missiles. It would also invite them to impose their own blockade on Berlin.

A blockade was also illegal. Under international law, no country was allowed to stop the ships of another in international waters. To skirt this legal issue, the president decided to call the blockade a "quarantine."

Kennedy refused to change his decision, which was supported by the majority of Ex-Comm members. When Kennedy met later with the Joint Chiefs, one of them admitted to the president that even a surprise attack could not be certain to destroy all the missile sites. Kennedy was now convinced that a blockade was the only justifiable option.

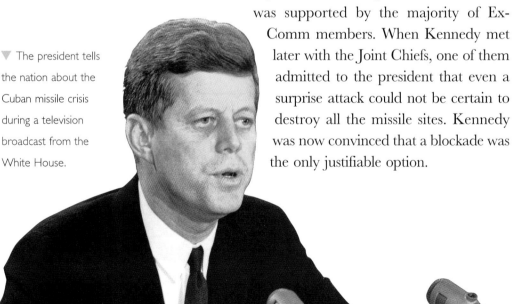

▼ The president tells the nation about the Cuban missile crisis during a television broadcast from the White House.

GETTING READY

Once the president made his decision, the military swung into action. The U.S. navy sent 180 ships to the Caribbean, while troops were moved to southern regions in the United States. Around the world, U.S. forces were put on alert.

At the same time, the United States contacted countries belonging to the North Atlantic Treaty Organization (NATO) and the Organization of American States (OAS) to inform them of the situation. All offered their support.

△ A U.S. naval destroyer sets out from its base in Puerto Rico to take part in the blockade of Cuba.

TELLING THE PUBLIC

On Monday evening, October 22, President Kennedy gave a nationally televised address from the White House. Millions of Americans watched the address, which was also broadcast on radio across Europe.

The president told a shocked public that the Soviets were installing offensive missiles on the "imprisoned island" of Cuba. He stressed that Khrushchev had lied repeatedly about the presence of such missiles. Kennedy then explained his decision to impose a U.S. quarantine on Cuba.

"The cost of freedom is always high," Kennedy said, "but Americans have always paid it. And one path we shall never choose, and that is the path of surrender or submission."

FRENCH SUPPORT

French president De Gaulle had this response upon seeing photographs of the Cuban missile bases:

"Tell President Kennedy, he must do what he has to do. And if this leads to World War Three, France will be with the United States."

As I Saw It by Dean Rusk

▲ Antiwar protesters take to the streets.

WORLD REACTIONS

People around the world were stunned by Kennedy's speech. Although Western heads of state all backed the United States, the reactions of private citizens varied greatly.

Anxiety about a possible nuclear holocaust had by then become widespread, as evidenced by the popular 1959 film *On the Beach*. Set in Australia after a global nuclear war, the film depicted a doomed group of people lining up for suicide pills as they waited for a slowly approaching radioactive cloud.

Kennedy's speech, therefore, incited alarm among many people. At Columbia University, Professor Richard Neustadt wrote that his students were "literally scared for their lives." Groups advocating for peace held demonstrations in Michigan and New York, where they carried signs saying "Hands off Cuba" and "We don't want to be nuked."

Other groups, however, called for even stronger U.S. action. In New York City's Madison Square Garden, 8,000 people who had gathered for an anti-Castro rally chanted "Fight! Fight! Fight!"

Opinion polls showed that the majority of Americans supported Kennedy. American newspapers had already warned the public about the Soviet military buildup in Cuba, and many people felt that U.S. action was long overdue.

Outside the United States, however, the blockade had much less support. Anti-U.S. riots erupted across Latin America, and in London thousands of demonstrators marched on the U.S. embassy, shouting "Viva Fidel! Kennedy to hell!"

British newspapers accused the United States of overreacting to the Soviet missiles in Cuba. For years, Britain and Western Europe had lived with the threat of Soviet missiles. Why couldn't the United States learn to live with the same danger?

REACTIONS TO THE CRISIS

Los Angeles grocer Sam Goldstad told a journalist about the panicked buying he witnessed in his shop:

"They're nuts. One lady's working four shopping carts at once. Another lady bought twelve packages of detergents. What's she going to do, wash up after the bomb?"

The only people who were pleased by Kennedy's speech were the Cuban émigrés. Sanchez Arango, an émigré leader, spoke on Miami television:

"This is the beginning of the end for Castro. We are very happy. The president is a wonderful man."

THE BRINK: CUBA, CASTRO AND JOHN F. KENNEDY BY DAVID DETZER

IN THE SOVIET UNION

Khrushchev was shocked by Kennedy's speech. His "missile gamble" had backfired in the worst possible way. According to Anatoly Dobrynin, Soviet ambassador to the United States, Khrushchev "had no fallback plan to deal with such a reverse" and was in a state of "total bewilderment."

On Tuesday afternoon, October 23, Radio Moscow broadcast news of the crisis. The U.S. blockade was presented as an act of unjustified aggression, and no mention was made of any Soviet missiles in Cuba.

To keep an outward appearance of calm, Khrushchev and the rest of the Soviet leadership went to an opera at the Bolshoi Theatre. Soviet citizens, however, knew that such an unusual event was a sure sign that a major crisis was under way.

CHAPTER SEVEN

The Blockade

Fidel Castro was aware of all the U.S. activity over the weekend. Even before Castro heard President Kennedy's speech on October 22, he began to call out the Cuban militia. Castro later recalled that he "understood by instinct, by smell, that something would happen."

For Castro and the Cuban people, a crisis had begun, not with Kennedy's speech but eighteen months earlier, with the Bay of Pigs invasion. The Cubans saw the Bay of Pigs as the start of an undeclared war that was being waged against them by the United States. Since November 1961, that war had continued in the form of the Operation Mongoose sabotage campaign.

▼ On the Havana waterfront, Cuban militiamen watch and wait for U.S. planes. They are armed with anti-aircraft guns.

READY TO DIE

General Sergio Del Valle, chief of staff of the Cuban Army, recalls the attitude of the Soviet troops stationed in Cuba:

"Our Soviet comrades at that stage were ready to fulfill the missions with us, to die alongside us, and they expressed this several times during our visits. It is absolutely certain that our Soviet brothers would die there with us."

BACK TO THE BRINK: PROCEEDINGS OF THE MOSCOW CONFERENCE ON THE CUBAN MISSILE CRISIS EDITED BY B. J. ALLEN, J. G. BLIGHT, AND D. A. WELCH

Soviet troops had little choice in the matter, as Soviet general Gribkov later explained:

"We had no way of leaving Cuba, no avenue for withdrawal."

WE NOW KNOW: RETHINKING COLD WAR HISTORY BY JOHN LEWIS GADDIS

Anxious marines at the U.S. base at Guantanamo Bay, Cuba, are briefed by their commander, General Collins. The base was reinforced with extra troops during the crisis. These soldiers expected that they might be attacked at any time.

The Cubans had been expecting an invasion for months, and they were now certain it would come. The U.S. naval blockade was considered a declaration of open war. Off the coast, Cubans saw the gathering U.S. war fleet, and every day they watched low-flying U.S. reconnaissance planes overhead.

MOBILIZATION

The whole country now readied itself for war, with 270,000 Cuban citizens mobilized. In Havana, major buildings were protected by barbed wire and sandbags. Anti-aircraft guns were set up in the squares, while tanks took to the streets.

Although Castro did not openly admit that he had nuclear missiles, he told the Cuban people that they now had the ability to destroy any aggressor. As a result, there was an atmosphere of defiance. Castro said that the Cuban people and their Soviet allies would fight to the last man.

CASTRO AND KHRUSHCHEV

Castro and Khrushchev communicated daily. The Cuban leader urged Khrushchev to keep firm and not bow down to the United States' demands. He claimed that Cuba was ready for the coming battle.

Khrushchev had never wanted to risk starting a war over Cuba. Now one of his greatest problems would be to hold Castro back.

CASTRO'S SUGGESTION

Castro's aggressive attitude alarmed Khrushchev, as he later recalled:

"Castro suggested that to prevent our nuclear missiles from being destroyed, we should launch a preemptive strike against the U.S. My comrades in the leadership and I realized that our friend Fidel totally failed to understand our purpose."

THE CUBAN MISSILE CRISIS REVISITED
EDITED BY JAMES NATHAN

"EYEBALL TO EYEBALL"

On the morning of Wednesday, October 24, two Soviet ships approached the quarantine line, accompanied by a Soviet submarine that had taken a position between them. The U.S. Navy had orders to intercept the ships and use depth charges if necessary to force the submarine to surface. If the ships refused to stop, the Navy had orders to open fire.

At 10:25 a.m., Kennedy was told that the Soviet ships had "stopped dead in the water." Khrushchev had made his first concession by ordering the ships not to cross the line. Secretary of State Dean Rusk commented, "We're eyeball to eyeball and I think the other fellow just blinked."

▼ Military positions for the U.S. blockade of Cuba.

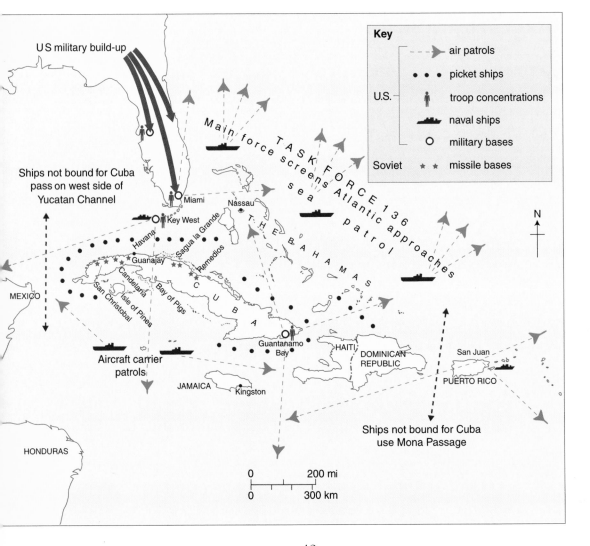

Despite Khrushchev's concession, the crisis was far from over. Aerial reconnaissance photographs showed that work on the missile sites had sped up and was now continuing day and night. For the first time, the photos also revealed Soviet jet bombers being assembled.

LETTERS

As the crisis continued, Kennedy and Khrushchev exchanged a series of letters, which were sent by cable in code and were then decoded and translated. Khrushchev's first letters were angry and defensive and accused the United States of piracy for its illegal blockade.

On October 26, however, a very different type of letter arrived from Khrushchev. At great length, he talked of the horrors of war, which he had seen firsthand. He said that Kennedy and he should not "pull on the ends of the rope in which you have tied the knots of war, because the more the two of us pull, the tighter the knot will be tied."

Khrushchev said he would not send arms to Cuba if Kennedy promised not to invade the island. Although he made no mention of the missiles already in place, his letter seemed to hold out hope of a solution to the crisis. For the first time, Kennedy felt cautiously optimistic that war could be avoided.

ROOM TO MOVE

Robert Kennedy recalled the president's words on not forcing Khrushchev to either fight or face humiliation:

"If anybody is around to write after this, they are going to understand that we made every effort to find peace and every effort to give our adversary room to move. I am not going to push the Russians an inch beyond what is necessary."

THIRTEEN DAYS BY ROBERT F. KENNEDY

BLACK SATURDAY

Despite Kennedy's newfound optimism, the following day, Saturday, October 27, proved to be the worst day of the whole crisis. It came to be known as "Black Saturday."

The first bad news arrived in the morning, when Khrushchev delivered a second, markedly different message to the United States over Radio Moscow. This public message was more formal than the private one, and Kennedy believed it was aimed at world opinion. Khrushchev now demanded the withdrawal of U.S. missiles in Turkey in exchange for the removal of Soviet "weapons" in Cuba.

The two different offers confused all the members of Ex-Comm. What was Khrushchev doing? Had hard-liners taken over in Moscow?

This offer also put Kennedy in a difficult position. The president had already decided to remove the missiles

◀ Major Rudolf Anderson, shot down by a Soviet missile, would be the only fatality of the Cuban crisis. After Castro ordered Anderson's body returned to the United States, Anderson was given a hero's burial. His wrecked plane ended up on display in a Cuban museum.

in Turkey; they were now considered obsolete and would be replaced with Polaris submarines. But if Kennedy agreed to Khrushchev's proposal, other countries would believe that the United States had traded Turkey's security for its own, and the whole NATO alliance would be undermined.

The Joint Chiefs of Staff had a simple explanation for Khrushchev's two contrasting offers: he was playing for time while the missiles in Cuba became operational. They drafted a formal recommendation that the president order a massive air strike for the next day, followed by a full invasion of Cuba.

THE FIRST SHOTS

Worse news arrived in the afternoon. Pilots returning from low-level reconnaissance flights reported that the Cubans had fired on them. Then came the report that Major Rudolf Anderson, the pilot who had first photographed the missile sites, had been brought down by a missile while flying his U-2 over the island. "The wreckage is on the ground," General Taylor told Kennedy, "and the pilot's dead."

Kennedy knew that the missiles in Cuba were under Soviet control. The shooting of the U-2 could only mean that either Khrushchev had chosen to escalate the crisis, or Soviet hard-liners had indeed taken over.

This news created a sense of urgency in the White House. The Joint Chiefs of Staff believed that they had been proven correct and urged the president to order a military strike.

A TIGHTENING NOOSE

In his memoir of the crisis, Robert Kennedy recalls the atmosphere in the White House as one piece of bad news followed another:

"There was the feeling that the noose was tightening on all of us, on Americans, on mankind, and all the bridges to escape were crumbling ... There was almost unanimous agreement that we had to attack early the next morning ..."

THIRTEEN DAYS BY ROBERT F. KENNEDY

A LAST CHANCE

Although war seemed close at hand, Kennedy decided to give Khrushchev one last chance for a peaceful solution. "We won't attack tomorrow," the president said. "We shall try again."

A new tactic was then devised by Robert Kennedy and Ted Sorenson, the president's speech writer. The president would ignore Khrushchev's second message demanding that U.S. missiles be removed from Turkey, and instead accept the terms of the first message. A letter was drafted for Kennedy in which he pledged not to invade Cuba if Khrushchev removed the Soviet missiles from the island. Once those weapons were removed, Kennedy would be willing to talk about "other armaments."

To impress Khrushchev with the urgency of the situation, the president asked his brother Bobby to visit Soviet ambassador Anatoly Dobrynin. He instructed Bobby to tell the ambassador that the missiles in Turkey would be withdrawn eventually, but that there could be no public announcement on the matter.

The president was wise to choose Bobby as a messenger. While John Kennedy was a reserved man with icy self-control, Robert Kennedy did not hide his feelings. His emotional state, at the end of the longest and worst day of the crisis, would impress Dobrynin as much as anything he might say. Bobby Kennedy's closeness to his brother also meant that his message would be taken as coming from the president.

Bobby told Dobrynin that time was running out. If Khrushchev did not agree to withdraw the missiles in a matter of hours, the situation was likely to spin out of control.

▲ The president's speech writer, Ted Sorenson, with his wife Sara. After Bobby Kennedy, Sorensen was Kennedy's closest and most trusted adviser.

46

Ambassador Dobrynin shares a joke with President Kennedy at their first meeting. His later talk with Bobby Kennedy would be decisive in ending the crisis.

In his memoirs, Anatoly Dobrynin described this meeting. Bobby Kennedy, he recalled, "remarked almost in passing that a lot of unreasonable people among American generals — and not only generals — were 'spoiling for a fight'... Throughout the whole meeting he was very nervous; indeed it was the first time I saw him in such a state."

In his own account of the crisis, Bobby Kennedy recalled the mood in the White House after the meeting. "The President was not optimistic, nor was I... What hope there was now rested with Khrushchev's revising his course within the next few hours. It was a hope, not an expectation. The expectation was a military confrontation by Tuesday and possibly tomorrow."

BOBBY'S TACTICS

In his meeting with Dobrynin, Bobby Kennedy hinted that the President might lose control of the U.S. military. According to Ex-Comm member Douglas Dillon, this was an effective tactic:

"It was a brilliant way to handle it.. I think he did a hell of a job convincing the Russians that the roof was going to fall in on the President.. That's what he was supposed to do, and he did it."

ON THE BRINK: AMERICANS AND SOVIETS RE-EXAMINE THE CUBAN MISSILE CRISIS
BY JAMES G. BLIGHT AND DAVID WELCH

THE VIEW FROM THE KREMLIN

With each passing day of the crisis, Khrushchev became more desperate to find a solution. By offering, on "Black Saturday," to remove Soviet missiles in Cuba if the United States removed its missiles in Turkey, he had not meant to place Kennedy in a difficult position. He was searching for a solution that would allow him to back down from the confrontation with dignity. His purpose in using a public broadcast was not to embarrass Kennedy, but to avoid the delay of a coded letter.

In his account of the crisis, Anatoly Dobrynin discussed Khrushchev's two different messages. "At first," Dobrynin explained, "he had been afraid to complicate the urgent search for settlement by insisting on the removal of American missiles from Turkey. But on second thought, under pressure from some of his colleagues, he made a desperate, last-minute attempt to obtain a deal to swap his missiles in Cuba for the American missiles."

The "Black Saturday" broadcast, however, confused Kennedy and infuriated both the Cubans and the Turks, who resented being treated as bargaining chips.

▼ Fidel Castro appeared utterly fearless and ready for war with the United States. His reckless attitude helped to convince Khrushchev that the missile crisis had to end.

LOSING CONTROL

Khrushchev was horrified by the downing of Major Anderson's U-2 plane. The Soviet premier had given no orders for U.S. planes to be fired upon. The order to shoot had came from Fidel Castro, who was convinced that a U.S. invasion of Cuba had already begun.

The U-2 plane was shot down by a Soviet general unsure of whose orders to follow. The general was far removed from Moscow and surrounded by hostile U.S. forces, which he believed Fidel Castro had already started firing upon. Even though the United States had not begun to invade, Castro's recklessness made a U.S. attack seem increasingly likely. In a moment of panic, the general gave the order to fire.

Khrushchev believed he was losing control of events in Cuba. The downing of the U-2 plane was proof that he could not even control his own troops. Now that the first shots had been fired, he knew the conflict was likely to escalate quickly.

The Soviet leader was already close to panic when Dobrynin reported his talk with Bobby Kennedy. Dobrynin gave the impression that the U.S. military might actually disregard Kennedy's authority and launch a full-scale war. The crisis had to be ended at once.

Khrushchev immediately agreed to remove the missiles in Cuba. He was so anxious to put a swift end to the crisis that he announced his agreement over Radio Moscow. He made no mention of the U.S. missiles in Turkey.

KHRUSHCHEV'S SPEECH

Dobrynin criticized the way Khrushchev ended the crisis with his radio broadcast:

"He was so confused that he did not play the one good card in his hand — Kennedy's agreement to withdraw U.S. missiles from Turkey. This could have been presented to the public as a deal trading their bases for ours ... Soviet citizens were stunned by the broadcast, for they had heard nothing official during the entire week about our missiles in Cuba."

IN CONFIDENCE BY ANATOLY DOBRYNIN

▼ This U.S. cartoon shows a terrified Khrushchev backing down while Kennedy holds firm.

'I've Changed My Mind, Let's Argue on the Bench'

CUBAN CRISIS

CHAPTER EIGHT

A Peaceful Solution?

▲ In August 1963, Nikita Khrushchev welcomes UN secretary general U Thant to Moscow for the signing of a treaty to ban nuclear tests.

Kennedy was careful not to claim that Khrushchev's agreement to remove Soviet missiles in Cuba was a victory for the United States. The president knew that Khrushchev had been placed in a difficult position, and he did not want to make it any worse for him.

Yet Kennedy could not stop the Western press from presenting the agreement as his own personal triumph. Previously, Kennedy had appeared to be a weak Cold War leader. He had been accused of lacking backbone during the Bay of Pigs invasion and of failing to stop the construction of the Berlin Wall. Now Kennedy had proved himself by standing up to Khrushchev and forcing the "Soviet bully" to back down. The public did not know about his agreement to withdraw U.S. missiles from Turkey.

The president was also praised for the way he had handled the crisis. He had kept his head throughout the thirteen days of the crisis, and he had refused to cave in to demands from the Joint Chiefs to launch an invasion. The successful outcome of the crisis was proof that Kennedy had made the right decisions.

WE ARE ALL MORTAL

On the day agreement on the Nuclear Test-Ban Treaty was reached, President Kennedy spoke to an audience of students at American University:

"Let us not be blind to our differences — but let us also direct attention to our common interests and to the means by which differences can be resolved … In the final analysis, our most basic common link is that we all inhabit this small planet. We all breathe the same air. We all cherish our children's future. And we are all mortal."

PUBLIC PAPERS OF THE PRESIDENTS

"WE'VE BEEN HAD!"

Not everyone in the United States viewed the end of the crisis as a victory. Cuban émigrés had been looking forward to returning home to a "free Cuba" and believed they had been let down again. The Joint Chiefs of Staff, who had been eager to attack Cuba, likewise considered Kennedy's promise not to invade the island as a failure of U.S. resolve.

On October 29, Kennedy called in the Joint Chiefs to thank them for their

support throughout the crisis. He was amazed at their attitude. "We've been had!" cried Admiral Anderson. General Curtis LeMay thumped a table and said, "It is the greatest defeat in our history, Mr. President…We should invade today!"

"The military," Kennedy later commented, "are mad."

▲ Kennedy smiles at the Dallas crowd, just moments before he is assassinated.

WORKING FOR PEACE

The Cuban missile crisis proved that neither the United States nor the Soviet Union wanted nuclear war. Since its resolution greatly increased Kennedy's authority as president, he decided to use his new position of strength to work towards better relations with Khrushchev and to reduce the nuclear threat. The result of Kennedy's efforts was a treaty banning nuclear tests, which in July 1963 Khrushchev agreed he would sign.

Just four months later, President Kennedy was killed in Dallas by an assassin's bullet.

▲ Chinese leader Mao (left) considered Nikita Khrushchev to be a weak and unworthy successor to the ruthless and iron-willed Joseph Stalin.

KHRUSHCHEV'S HUMILIATION

On "Black Saturday," Khrushchev had publicly called on the United States to withdraw its missiles from Turkey. Yet the following day, in his second Radio Moscow broadcast, he offered to remove Soviet missiles from Cuba without even mentioning U.S. missiles in Turkey.

Khrushchev claimed that he had secured the safety of Socialist Cuba. Soviet citizens, however, clearly understood that Khrushchev's failure to win concessions on U.S. missiles in Turkey was a humiliating public defeat for the Soviet leader. He brought the world to the brink of nuclear war but gained almost nothing.

Khrushchev knew that he had been beaten. Red-faced when he announced his deal with Kennedy to his colleagues, he reportedly said, "Comrades, Lenin's cause is lost."

A PERSONAL TRIUMPH

In his memoirs, Khrushchev tried to cast a positive light on his decision to remove missiles in Cuba:

"The Caribbean crisis was a triumph of Soviet foreign policy and a personal triumph in my own career as a statesman… We achieved, I would say, a spectacular success without having to fire a single shot!… It cost us nothing more than the round-trip expenses for transporting the rockets to Cuba and back."

KHRUSHCHEV REMEMBERS BY NIKITA KHRUSHCHEV

CHINA

One of the primary reasons for installing missiles in Cuba had been to boost Soviet prestige and impress the Chinese, but the end of the crisis achieved the opposite effect. In Khrushchev's words, Chinese radio "started hooting and shouting about how Khrushchev had turned coward and backed down." Chinese radio also broadcast the charge that Khrushchev was not fit to be world communist leader.

Until the missile crisis, Khrushchev had managed to restrain the Chinese from building their own nuclear bombs. Now, however, Mao claimed that communist countries could no longer rely on the Soviet Union for their defense. Mao decided that China needed its own nuclear weapons.

The Chinese successfully detonated their first nuclear bomb on October 16, 1964. Just two days earlier, Nikita Khrushchev had fallen from power.

Leonid Brezhnev spent a year gathering support for a plot against Nikita Khrushchev. He finally overthrew him in October 1964.

KHRUSHCHEV'S FALL

Khrushchev's position as Soviet leader was damaged by the crisis. Although his personal authority was still too great for him to be challenged in 1962, his colleagues had begun to lose patience with his reckless style of leadership.

When they finally did conspire against him, two years later, the first charge they leveled against Khrushchev was one of "hasty and ill-considered decisions." They replaced Khrushchev with Leonid Brezhnev, who would ultimately prove to be the most cautious of all the Soviet leaders.

A PAWN

In 1963, Castro talked with a French journalist:

"Cuba does not want to be a pawn on the world's chessboard … I cannot agree with Khrushchev promising Kennedy to return the missiles without making the least reference to the indispensable approval of the Cuban government."

KENNEDY V. KHRUSHCHEV, THE CRISIS YEARS
BY MICHAEL R. BESCHLOSS

CUBA BETRAYED

Fidel Castro learned about the agreement between Khrushchev and Kennedy by listening to the radio. Khrushchev had not even consulted him about the negotiations. Castro was furious; he kicked a wall and smashed a mirror. He reportedly claimed that, if he could, he would have beaten Khrushchev to within an inch of his life.

Castro had devoted his life to Cuba's struggle for independence and dignity,

From 1965 to 1967, Ernesto "Che" Guevara launched a series of unsuccessful revolutionary wars to spread communism. He was captured and executed in Bolivia in 1967. This picture of Che made him an icon of youthful rebellion in the 1960s and the 1970s.

VIVA CHE

freeing his country from the foreign dominance of the United States. Now the Soviets were acting as if Cuba belonged to them. Castro was particularly angered by Khrushchev's agreement to allow United Nations inspectors to visit Cuba, in order to verify that the Soviet missiles had been withdrawn.

CASTRO'S DEMANDS

Castro made his own demands before agreeing to the UN inspection. He called on the United States to end its campaign of sabotage against Cuba, to close down its training camps for Cuban émigrés, and to surrender its naval base at Cuba's Guantanamo Bay. If the UN inspected the United States' Cuban-émigré training camps, Castro said, then UN inspectors would be allowed in Cuba. Otherwise, he warned, "Whoever comes to inspect Cuba must come armed for battle!"

Although the missiles were removed, Castro's hostile stance allowed Kennedy to skirt his pledge not to invade Cuba. The CIA's secret war on Cuba continued, resulting in more factories bombed and more assassination attempts on Castro. An economic blockade was also imposed on Cuba, one that is still in force today, forty years later.

As Castro said of the crisis, "War was avoided, but peace was not gained."

SPREADING COMMUNISM

Castro believed that he could not depend on the Soviets to defend Cuba. To create

CHE GUEVARA

Ernesto "Che" Guevara, the leading figure in Castro's international guerrilla campaigns for communism, described the scope of the struggle against "Yankee imperialism":

"U.S. imperialism is guilty of aggression — its crimes are enormous and cover the whole world … It must be defeated in a world confrontation … To die under the flag of Vietnam, of Venezuela, of Guatemala, of Laos, of Guinea, of Colombia, of Bolivia, of Brazil — to name only a few scenes of today's armed struggle — would be equally glorious and desirable for an American, an Asian, an African, even a European."

VENCEREMOS! THE SPEECHES AND WRITINGS OF CHE GUEVARA
EDITED BY JOHN GERASSI

new alliances and widen his struggle against the United States, he stepped up his efforts to spread communism to Latin America and elsewhere in the Third World.

SECRET TALKS

While Kennedy remained publicly hostile to Castro, in private he attempted a new approach. Recently published documents reveal that, in the last months of his life, Kennedy began secret talks with Castro, in order to find a way to normalize relations with Cuba. Kennedy hoped to use Castro's anger towards Khrushchev to entice the Cuban leader away from his Soviet alliance. Castro welcomed the approach, which was unfortunately cut short by Kennedy's death.

55

CHAPTER NINE

Lessons of the Crisis

The Cuban missile crisis ended the Cold War's second phase, which had been characterized by dramatic crises. The leaders of the United States and the Soviet Union now tried to avoid direct confrontations.

Both Kennedy and Khrushchev were alarmed by how close the two superpowers had come to nuclear war. One of their first acts after the crisis was to install a telephone link, called the "hotline," between Soviet headquarters and the White House. By communicating directly, the leaders hoped to avoid misunderstandings that might lead to war.

▼ U.S. soldiers in action during the Vietnam War.

VIETNAM

The successful outcome of the Cuban missile crisis gave the United States increased confidence as a superpower and led to its willingness to take on a wider global military role. In 1965, Kennedy's successor, President Lyndon Johnson, launched a massive bombing campaign against communist North Vietnam. Soon, 50,000 U.S. troops were fighting in Vietnam. The Vietnam conflict lasted until 1973, and became the longest war ever fought by the United States.

PEACE MOVEMENTS

Many people in the West believed that the successful outcome of the missile crisis proved the necessity of nuclear weapons. The threat of a nuclear holocaust, they argued, forced both Khrushchev and Kennedy to draw back from war.

This attitude was a blow to anti-nuclear groups, not only in the United States but abroad. For instance, starting in 1958 thousands of antinuclear demonstrators marched annually on a weapons research center in Britain, but the last big march was held in 1963.

The 1960s would prove to be a decade full of antiwar protests. Millions of demonstrators, mostly young people, took to the streets of the United States and Europe. For the most part, however, they demonstrated not against the proliferation of nuclear weapons but against the long, bloody, and conventional war fought by the United States in Vietnam.

KHRUSHCHEV ON KENNEDY

In his memoirs, Khrushchev gave this assessment of President Kennedy:

"His death was a great loss. He was gifted with the ability to resolve international conflicts by negotiation, as the whole world learned during the so-called Cuban crisis. Regardless of his youth, he was a real statesman. I believe that if Kennedy had lived, relations between the Soviet Union and the United States would be much better than they are. Why do I say that? Because Kennedy would have never let his country get bogged down in Vietnam."

KHRUSHCHEV REMEMBERS BY NIKITA KHRUSHCHEV

CONTINUING COLD WAR

The Cuban missile crisis had dramatically exposed Soviet weaknesses. When it was over, Soviet deputy foreign minister V. V. Kuznetsov said, "Never will we be caught like this again."

In his last two years of power, Khrushchev was forced to give in to pressure from the Soviet military to increase spending on nuclear weapons. This was a bitter blow. Khrushchev had dreamed of improving the living standards of the Soviet people. Now submarines and missiles would take priority, as the Soviet Union sought to match the United States in the arms race.

STAGNATION

Under Leonid Brezhnev, the Soviet Union became a true military superpower, with a nuclear arsenal as massive as that of the United States. Yet the price of this military buildup was economic inefficiency, bad housing, food shortages, and a discontented population.

If Khrushchev had been an idealist, Brezhnev was a cynic who did not really believe in communism. "All that stuff about communism," he confided in his brother, "is a tall tale for popular consumption."

▼ In the 1990s, the loss of Soviet oil imports forced Cuba to open its own oil fields. Between 1991 and 2000, Cuban oil production increased from 8,630 to 44,800 barrels a day.

The Brezhnev era, which lasted from 1964 to 1982, would later be known as the "era of stagnation." The government's failure to win public support would be a major factor in the eventual collapse of the Soviet system in 1989 to 1991.

CASTRO TODAY

In 1991, as the Soviet Union crumbled, the Russians announced the withdrawal of their 11,000 military advisers and technicians from Cuba. At that time, Cuba's trade with Eastern bloc countries likewise disappeared.

The loss of Soviet subsidies was a disaster for Castro. In 1993, he announced that Cubans would be able to own U.S. dollars. Two years later, he allowed foreign companies to own Cuban property and open businesses. Old class differences reemerged, since Cubans with U.S. dollars now had access to better goods.

Despite Castro's concessions to capitalism, the United States remained hostile to Cuba and even tightened its economic blockade of the island. To keep foreign companies from investing in Cuba, in 1996 President Clinton signed the "Helms-Burton Bill," which gave U.S. companies the right to sue any businesses making use of their confiscated property in Cuba.

Despite forty years of opposition from the world's most powerful nation, Fidel Castro has survived, becoming the world's longest-serving political leader. At the start of the twenty-first century, Castro's Cuba is the last country still fighting the Cold War with the United States.

▲ Fidel Castro has lived to see the worldwide collapse of communism, but he has held on to both power and his faith in his political system.

WAITING FOR THE TRAIN TO MOVE

A Russian joke compares the leadership styles of three Cold War-era Soviet rulers:

"Stalin, Khrushchev, and Brezhnev were sitting on a train in a station, getting increasingly worried that it refused to move.

Stalin said, 'Let's shoot one of the drivers. That would scare the others and make them start the train.'

'That would be wrong,' said Khrushchev. 'We must raise the drivers' salaries and encourage them to get the train moving.'

Brezhnev said, 'Why don't we just close the curtains, and pretend that the train is moving?'"

Time Line

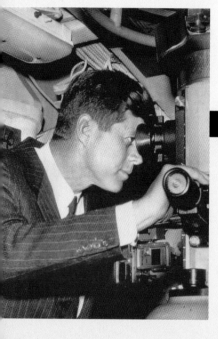

1952

NOVEMBER 1
United States explodes hydrogen bombs on Elugelab Island in the Pacific Ocean

1953

MARCH 5
Stalin dies

1957

JULY
Khrushchev defeats his rivals to become the new Soviet leader

OCTOBER 4
Soviets launch the satellite *Sputnik* into space

1961

JANUARY 20
John F. Kennedy takes office as president of the United States

APRIL 12
Soviet cosmonaut Yuri Gagarin makes first manned spaceflight

APRIL 14-19
Invading army of U.S.-backed Cuban émigrés defeated at the Bay of Pigs

JUNE 3
Kennedy and Khrushchev meet in Vienna

AUGUST 12
East Germans begin construction of Berlin Wall

NOVEMBER
Kennedy approves "Operation Mongoose," the secret war against Castro's regime

OCTOBER 28
Khrushchev agrees to remove all Soviet missiles from Cuba

1959

JANUARY 1
Fidel Castro comes to power
in Cuba

MAY 17
Castro begins seizure of
U.S.-owned land in Cuba

1960

FEBRUARY 13
Castro signs a trade agreement
with the Soviet Union

1962

OCTOBER 15
Spy photographs reveal the
presence of Soviet missile
sites in Cuba

OCTOBER 22
Kennedy announces a
"quarantine" of Cuba

OCTOBER 24
Soviet ships turn back from the
quarantine line

OCTOBER 27
("Black Saturday")
Khrushchev demands withdrawal
of U.S. missiles in Turkey;
U-2 spy plane is shot down
over Cuba

1963

JULY 25
Kennedy and Khrushchev agree
on Nuclear Test-Ban Treaty

NOVEMBER 22
President Kennedy assassinated
in Dallas, Texas

1964

OCTOBER 14
Khrushchev falls from power

OCTOBER 16
China explodes a nuclear bomb

Glossary

atomic bomb: earliest form of nuclear weapon, based on nuclear fission.

ballistic missile: missile that reaches the top of its arc with rocket power and then falls freely to its target.

blockade: tactic of isolating an area by blocking all approaches to it.

capitalism: ideology and economic system based on individual ownership of property and a free, competitive market that determines prices and wages.

CIA: acronym for Central Intelligence Agency, established in 1947 to manage U.S. foreign intelligence operations.

Cold War: rivalry between the United States and the Soviet Union, as well as their respective allies, that lasted between 1945 and 1991.

communism: ideology that advocates government owning all property and controlling the economy in order to create a classless society, and which usually involves authoritarian rule.

Ex-Comm: abbreviation for Executive Committee of the National Security Council, a group of advisers assembled by President Kennedy during the Cuban missile crisis.

guerrilla: type of warfare that involves small, mobile groups of soldiers.

hydrogen bomb: nuclear weapon, based on nuclear fusion, that has far more destructive power than an atomic bomb.

ICBM: acronym for intercontinental ballistic missile, a long-range weapon with a range of more than 3,400 miles (5,470 km).

ideology: belief or way of thinking, as in a communist or capitalist ideology.

Joint Chiefs of Staff: head officers of the various branches of the U.S. military.

military-industrial complex: powerful alliance of the U.S. military and the U.S. defense industry.

nationalize: convert privately owned property or business to state ownership.

NATO: acronym for North Atlantic Treaty Organization, a defensive alliance of Western nations established in 1949.

nuclear deterrence: stalemate between the United States and the Soviet Union based on each side's unwillingness to risk nuclear annihilation.

Nuclear Test-Ban Treaty: treaty first signed on August 5, 1963, by the United States, the Soviet Union, and Britain that banned almost all forms of nuclear testing.

OAS: acronym for Organization of American States, an alliance of nations in the Western hemisphere established in 1948.

Operation Mongoose: secret CIA-backed campaign in the 1960s that sought to undermine Castro's regime through sabotage and other acts.

Polaris: U.S. submarine developed in 1960 that could launch nuclear missiles.

strategic nuclear weapon: long-range nuclear weapon, usually targeted at cities or military installations.

tactical nuclear weapon: short-range nuclear weapon, for use in battle.

U-2: U.S. spy plane, developed in 1955, that could fly at high altitude and take detailed aerial photographs.

United Nations: organization of nations first established in 1945 to safeguard world peace and foster international cooperation.

Books

Anatomy of the Cuban Missile Crisis (Guides to Historic Events of the Twentieth Century series)
James A. Nathan (Greenwood Press)

The Cuban Missile Crisis (World History series)
Catherine Hester Gow (Lucent Books)

The Kennedy Tapes: Inside the White House During the Cuban Missile Crisis
Ernest R. May and Philip D. Zelikow (Harvard University Press)

Missiles in Cuba: Kennedy, Khrushchev, and Castro and the 1962 Crisis
Mark J. White (Ivan R. Dee)

Thirteen Days: A Memoir of the Cuban Missile Crisis Robert F. Kennedy (W.W. Norton & Company)

Videos

20th Century with Mike Wallace: Bay of Pigs / Cuban Missile Crisis
(A & E Home Video)

CNN Perspectives Presents: The Cold War
(Turner Home Video)

Cuban Missile Crisis: A Spy Talks
(Goldhil Home Video)

Cuban Missile Crisis: Thirteen Days in October
(Goldhil Home Video)

The Missiles of October
(MPI Home Video)

Thirteen Days
(New Line Studios)

Web Sites

14 Days in October: The Cuban Missile Crisis
library.thinkquest.org/11046

Berlin Wall Online
www.dailysoft.com/berlinwall/ index.html

The Real Thirteen Days: The Hidden History of the Cuban Missile Crisis
www.gwu.edu/~nsarchiv/nsa/ cuba_mis_cri

Index